How to carve a pumpkin

OH MY GOURD!

plus 29 other fun
Halloween activities

Jack Hallow

How to carve a *pumpkin*

OH MY GOURD!

plus 29 other fun
Halloween activities

Jack Hallow

**Smith
Street
Books**

HOW TO CARVE A PUMPKIN

Here's a scoop: gourds can be turned into just about any dish you can imagine. Boil 'em, mash 'em, stick 'em in a stew. Although, whether you've got a pumpkin, winter squash or a calabash, there's one thing you can do with these fruits that beats anything you can cook. (Yes, they're fruit.)

Carving a jack-o'-lantern is a time-honoured tradition once fall rolls around. The pastime is slowly creeping its way around the world, as Halloween is celebrated by more people in more countries with each passing year. So, here's a little refresher.

Welcome to Gourd Carving 101.

STEP 1: PREPARE

Acquire your gourd of choice. These can be found in places as whimsical as a pumpkin patch, or as fluorescent and soulless as a supermarket. You'll want to avoid any gourd too short or squat. Also make sure you've got a small(ish) serrated knife on hand.

STEP 2: BEHEAD

You'll start by removing the crown. Using the knife, stab a wide circle around the stem (technically the "peduncle") of your gourd. Pry this crown off as you would the lid to a can of Pringles and set aside for later.

STEP 3: DISEMBOWEL

Using a spoon, ladle or your bare animalistic hands, remove the insides of your gourd. Don't discard the seeds, fibre and flesh, as you'll find plenty of ways to use every last ounce. Nose to tail, if you will.

STEP 4: VANDALISE

Now, here's your chance to get creative. Whip out a marker and sketch your design out on one half of the gourd's exterior wall. This might be the spooky face of a former lover, the lyrics to your favourite ABBA track, or one of the stencils included at the end of this book! Whatever you fancy, opt for big and chunky shapes that will prove easy to carve.

STEP 5: PIERCE

Carefully, with the blade's edge always facing away from your precious fingers and whatever else, get stabbing. Pierce the gourd's hull and cut along your hand-drawn design, pulling chunks out to reveal the image's silhouette.

STEP 6: YOU'RE DONE!

Finally, plonk your creation on the front stoop –
or somewhere equally triumphant – and place
a battery-powered LED light inside its corpse.
Replace the crown atop the gourd's head and enjoy
the creepy glow of your very own jack-o'-lantern.

THINGS TO EAT

BREAKFAST SMOOTHIE

Is a smoothie topped with granola still, in its very essence, a smoothie? These are the kind of existential questions you can ponder as the blender is running and you're making this balanced autumnal breakfast.

✗   ✗

Serves 2

250 ml (1 cup) milk

125 g (½ cup) plain yoghurt

1 small banana

1 tablespoon maple syrup

¼ teaspoon ground cinnamon

55 g (½ cup) granola of your choice (optional)

80 g (½ cup) blueberries (optional)

Pumpkin puree
1 pumpkin (winter squash), approximately 1.5 to 2.6 kg (sugar pumpkin, butternut pumpkin or other pumpkin of your choice)

salt (optional)

First, make the pumpkin puree. As a general rule, 1 kg (2 lb 3 oz) of pumpkin will make 500 g (2 cups) of puree.

Preheat the oven to 200°C (400°F). Line a large baking tray with baking paper.

Cut the pumpkin in half, from stem to base. Scoop out the fibres and seeds, putting the seeds aside for another use. If you'll use the puree for a savoury dish, you can add a sprinkle of salt to the cut sides. Place the two halves cut-side down onto the baking tray.

Transfer to the oven and roast for 50–60 minutes, until the flesh is soft and can be pierced easily with a knife. Remove from the oven. When cool, scoop the flesh from the skin and place into a food processor. Process until smooth, then transfer to an air-tight container until ready to use.

To make the smoothie, place the milk, yoghurt, banana, maple syrup, ground cinnamon and 125 g (½ cup) of the pumpkin puree into a blender. Blend until smooth. Divide the smoothie between 2 glasses, and garnish with the granola and blueberries.

The puree will keep in the fridge for 5 days, and in the freezer for 3 months.

PUMPKIN SEED GRANOLA

After making your own, store-bought granola tastes like trash. Trash laced with bland crunchy bits and no soul. If you haven't DIY-ed granola before, this recipe with honey, oats, goji berries, pumpkin seeds and cinnamon is a great place to start.

Makes 3 cups

200 g (2 cups) rolled oats

60 g (½ cup) pumpkin seeds

40 g (⅓ cup) goji berries

30 g (¼ cup) sunflower seeds

30 g (½ cup) shredded coconut

pinch of salt

90 g (¼ cup) honey

60 ml (¼ cup) coconut oil

1 teaspoon vanilla extract

Pumpkin pie spice

1 tablespoon ground cinnamon

1 teaspoon ground ginger

1 teaspoon ground nutmeg

½ teaspoon ground cloves

Make the pumpkin spice mix by combining the ingredients in a small bowl. Transfer to a small jar, adding a label with the name and date on it for convenience.

Preheat the oven to 180°C (350°F). Line a baking tray with baking paper.

To make the granola, place all the dry ingredients and 2 teaspoons of the pumpkin spice mix into a bowl and mix well to combine.

If needed, heat the honey and coconut oil for about 5–7 seconds in the microwave, until it's very runny, then add it along with the vanilla extract to the bowl. Mix well so that the dry ingredients are coated by the wet ingredients.

Spread the granola out in an even layer onto the prepared baking tray. Place in the oven and bake for 20–30 minutes, taking out of the oven and stirring every 10 minutes to keep it loose. Remove from the oven and leave to cool.

Store the granola in an airtight container for up to 2 weeks.

The spice mix will keep for up to 6 months.

PUMPKIN SPICED WAFFLES

What's the only thing better on this big, beautiful planet than pancakes? Yes, correct, it's waffles. Pillow-soft with just the slightest crunch on the outside, these PSL-y waffles might have to become a year-round tradition.

✖   ✖

Makes 10–12

300 g (2 cups) plain (all-purpose) flour

55 g (¼ cup) brown sugar

2 teaspoons Pumpkin pie spice (see page 12)

1 teaspoon baking powder

½ teaspoon baking soda

¼ teaspoon salt

340 ml (1⅓ cup) milk

3 eggs

250 g (1 cup) Pumpkin puree, fresh (see page 11) or tinned

60 ml (¼ cup) maple syrup

3 tablespoons vegetable oil

honey, to serve (optional)

Preheat a waffle iron.

Place the flour, sugar, pumpkin pie spice, baking powder, baking soda and salt in a bowl and stir to combine.

In a separate bowl, place the milk, eggs, pumpkin puree, maple syrup and vegetable oil and and whisk until the mixture is well combined.

Pour the wet ingredients into the dry ingredients and mix until just combined.

Pour about 90 g (⅓ cup) of the waffle batter into each waffle plate. Close the lid and cook until golden brown and slightly crispy around the edges.

Serve with honey, if you like.

PUMPKIN CHIPS

The potato will always remain the OG starch-based chip. But if you need to convince your significant other that there's a healthy alternative – pumpkin chips might be your decoy. They're not better for you, but they *are* orange. So, there's that.

x   x

Makes 1 large bowl

250 g (9 oz) pumpkin (winter squash), peeled and trimmed

vegetable oil, for deep frying

Thyme salt

2 tablespoons salt flakes

2 teaspoons fresh thyme leaves

zest of 1 lemon

First, make the thyme salt. Preheat the oven to 140°C (275°F). Combine the ingredients in a small bowl, mixing with your fingers to crush everything together. Spread the mixture on a small baking tray, then transfer to the oven, at the same time turning the oven off. Leave for 2–3 hours, then transfer to a small airtight container.

Layer a baking tray with paper towel and set aside.

To make the chips, use a mandolin or vegetable peeler to cut the pumpkin into very thin slices, then lay them on a clean, dry dish cloth. Use a second cloth to pat them dry.

Heat the oil to around 190°C (375°F), or until a cube of bread turns golden brown after 10 seconds in the oil. In batches, fry the pumpkin until crisp, which should take between 1 and 3 minutes, depending on how thin they have been sliced. Remove from the oil with a slotted spoon, place on the paper towel and sprinkle over some thyme salt while they are still hot. Serve immediately.

Leftover salt will keep for 3 months in an airtight container.

PUMPKIN HUMMUS

This silky hummus is prime for the dipping. Whether your weapon of choice is pita bread, fresh falafel, any manner of veggie stick or even the humble human finger, hummus is universal.

✕ ✕

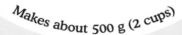

Makes about 500 g (2 cups)

400 g (14 oz) peeled and cleaned pumpkin (winter squash), cut into 2 cm (¾ in) cubes

1 tablespoon olive oil, plus more for drizzling

1 head garlic

400 g (14 oz) tinned chickpeas, drained and rinsed

juice of ½ lemon

90 g (⅓ cup) tahini

1 teaspoon kosher salt

1 teaspoon ground cumin

½ teaspoon chilli powder (optional)

1 tablespoon toasted peanuts

2 sage leaves, thinly sliced

Preheat the oven to 180°C (350°F).

Place the pumpkin in a roasting tin and drizzle over the tablespoon of olive oil. Break up the garlic head and toss the cloves in the tin, then season everything with salt and cracked black pepper. Roast in the oven for 20–25 minutes, until the pumpkin is soft. Remove from the oven and allow to cool slightly.

Place the pumpkin into the bowl of a food processor. Squeeze the garlic flesh from the skins, and add to the bowl, along with the chickpeas, lemon juice, tahini, salt, cumin and chilli powder, if using. Turn the processor on, then with the motor running, slowly add up to 125 ml (½ cup) cold water. Check the texture as you go, stopping when it reaches your desired texture.

Transfer to a serving bowl and garnish with the toasted peanuts, sliced sage and a drizzle of olive oil.

THE DEVIL'S EGGS

These ain't your mommy's devilled eggs.
Bulked up with pumpkin, peppers and chilli,
these bad boys pack a spicy punch. You have been
warned, as you should warn your guests when
they start circling this devilish platter.

✗ ✗

Serves a crowd

8 eggs

60 g (¼ cup) whole-egg
mayonnaise

60 g (¼ cup) Pumpkin
puree, fresh (see page 11)
or tinned

1 tablespoon Dijon
mustard

1 teaspoon white vinegar

1–2 drops liquid smoke
(optional)

smoked paprika, to
garnish

¼ red capsicum (bell
pepper), cut into small
triangles

1 large mild red chilli,
cut into small triangles
(optional)

Fill a medium-sized saucepan with water, then place over a high heat. Once the water is boiling, use a spoon to gently lower the eggs into the water. Reduce heat slightly, to a gentle boil, and set a timer for 9 minutes. Once the time is up, place the eggs into an ice bath until cool (alternatively, you can place them under running cold water).

Peel the eggs, then slice each in half. Gently remove the yolks and place them into a bowl. In the same bowl, add the mayonnaise, pumpkin puree, mustard, vinegar and liquid smoke (if using) to the yolks, season with salt and freshly ground black pepper, then mash to a smooth paste.

Spoon the mixture into a piping bag, then pipe mixture into the egg white halves. Sprinkle with paprika and stick a few bits of capsicum and chilli into the piped mixture – omit the chilli if your guests are heat shy!

PUMPKIN SOUP

The fountain of youth and the place I most want to dip my crouton: pumpkin soup is the GOAT of the Stew Culinary Universe. When served in a hollowed-out gourd, everyone's favourite starter takes on a whole other dimension. Come on in, the soup's fine.

✗   ✗

Serves 6

3 small pumpkins (winter squash), such as sugar or pie pumpkins

2 tablespoons olive oil, plus more for rubbing

1 onion, roughly chopped

2 garlic cloves

1 teaspoon ground cumin

½ teaspoon chilli powder (optional)

1 kg (2 lb 3 oz) pumpkin (winter squash), peeled and cut into chunks

750 ml (3 cups) stock of your choosing

125 ml (½ cup) cream

pumpkin seeds, chilli flakes and thyme, to garnish

To make a pumpkin bowl, preheat the oven to 180°C (350°C). Line a baking tray with baking paper. Slice the pumpkins in half lengthways through the stem. Use a spoon to remove the seeds. Depending on the size of the cavity, you might need to hollow out a bit of the flesh.

Transfer to the baking tray, cut-side up – if the pumpkins don't sit flat on the tray, slice off a small slice to ensure they sit evenly. Rub a little olive oil inside each cavity, then transfer to the oven to cook for about 15 minutes – they should be tender but not so soft that they collapse. Set aside and keep warm.

Meanwhile, heat the oil in a heavy-based saucepan over a medium heat. Add the onion and cook for 5 to 6 minutes, stirring often, until translucent but not browned. Add the garlic, cumin and chilli powder (if using) and cook for a further minute, then add the pumpkin and stock and bring to the boil. Boil for 15 to 20 minutes, until the pumpkin is completely tender.

Use a stick bender to puree the soup, then stir in the cream.

Transfer the pumpkin halves to plates, ladle some soup into each half, then scatter over the pumpkin seeds, chilli flakes and thyme. Serve immediately.

PUMPKIN RAVIOLI

"When the moon hits your soul-y like pumpkin ravioli, *that's amore.*" The ancient Italian proverb seems as true today as it was when it was written – as you'll discover upon biting into one of these feta-pumped, sage-butter-soaked beauties.

Serves 4–6

Pasta

150 g (1 cup) plain (all-purpose) flour, plus extra for dusting

165 g (1 cup) fine semolina flour

1 egg, plus 5 egg yolks, lightly beaten

1 tablespoon water

Filling

250 g (1 cup) Pumpkin puree, fresh (see page 11) or tinned

60 g (2 oz) feta, crumbled

30 g (1 oz) parmesan, finely grated

2 teaspoons lemon zest

1 egg yolk

Sauce

200 g (7 oz) butter

30 sage leaves

Place the pasta ingredients into the bowl of a food processor and blitz until it resembles breadcrumbs. Turn out onto a floured surface, then knead for 5–7 minutes until smooth. Wrap it in plastic wrap and rest it for 30 minutes.

Meanwhile, place the filling ingredients into a bowl. Season with salt and pepper then mix until combined. Set aside.

Working with a quarter of the dough at a time, pass the dough through a pasta machine, working from the widest setting to the thinnest. Lay the pasta on a floured surface and cover with a towel while you work with the next batch.

Cut one pasta sheet in half lengthways, then place 2 teaspoons of the filling at 4 cm (1½ in) intervals down the middle of the dough. Brush water around the edges then lay the other pasta strip on top, gently pressing down to enclose your filling. Cut each filled piece into squares, then transfer to a floured tray while you make the remaining ravioli. Bring a large saucepan of salted water to the boil and cook the ravioli in batches for 7–8 minutes, until al dente, then remove with a slotted spoon to serving bowls.

Melt the butter in a frying pan over medium heat until it begins to foam and turn golden brown. Add the sage leaves and fry until crisp, then spoon the sauce over the pasta.

PUMPKIN RISOTTO

Load your guests up with this carb-loaded bowl of pumpkin, rice and parmesan. A few artfully placed sprigs of rosemary on top does more than look classy, this pop of flavour really puts the OH in risotto.

Serves 4

600 g (1 lb 5 oz) butternut or kent pumpkin (winter squash), peeled and cut into 2 cm (¾ in) chunks

2½ tablespoons olive oil

1.25 litres (5 cups) vegetable or chicken stock

75 g (2¾ oz) butter

1 onion, finely chopped

2 large garlic cloves, finely chopped

1 bay leaf

2 thyme sprigs

330 g (1½ cups) arborio rice

125 ml (½ cup) dry white wine

50 g (½ cup) finely grated parmesan

A few rosemary sprigs

Preheat the oven to 170°C (340°F). Line a baking tray with baking paper.

Put the pumpkin in a large bowl. Drizzle with 1½ tablespoons of the olive oil, sprinkle generously with sea salt flakes and freshly ground black pepper and toss to combine. Place on the lined baking tray and roast for 30 minutes, or until golden.

Pour the stock into a saucepan and bring just to the boil. Turn off the heat.

In a large shallow saucepan or deep frying pan, heat the remaining olive oil and a third of the butter. Cook the onion over low heat for 5 minutes. Add the garlic, bay leaf, thyme sprigs and rice, stirring to coat the rice in the oil.

Stir in the wine. Gradually add the hot stock, a ladleful at a time, stirring until the stock has been almost absorbed. Keep adding the stock gradually, cooking over low heat.

Stir in the pumpkin with the last addition of stock, mashing about half the pumpkin lightly with a fork as you add it. Remove the bay leaf and thyme sprigs, discarding the bay leaf, and stripping the leaves off the thyme and adding them back into the risotto. Taste the rice to ensure it is cooked then stir through the parmesan and remaining butter. Serve garnished with rosemary sprigs, if you like.

PUMPKIN SEED LOAF

Remember when everyone got obsessed with baking sourdough? It's time to leave those boring, white blobs back in lockdown where they belong. This bread rises from pumpkin puree and is guaranteed to never remind you of 2020.

✗   ✗

Makes 1 loaf

150 g (1 cup) plain (all-purpose) flour

¼ teaspoon salt

½ teaspoon baking powder

¼ teaspoon baking soda

½ teaspoon cinnamon

½ teaspoon nutmeg

80 g (2¾ oz) butter, softened, plus extra for greasing

115 g (½ cup) brown sugar

110 g (½ cup) sugar

1 egg

220 g (8 oz) Pumpkin puree, fresh (see page 11) or tinned

30 g (¼ cup) chopped pecans

1 tablespoon pumpkin seeds

Preheat the oven to 140°C (275°F) and grease a 4-cup capacity loaf tin with butter.

Place the flour, salt, baking powder and soda and spices into a bowl then stir to combine.

Place the butter and sugars into a separate bowl and use an electric mixer to beat until combined. Add the egg and mix for 1–2 minutes until fully incorporated and the mixture has lightened in colour. Add the pumpkin puree and beat for a further 30 seconds. Add the flour mixture and mix on a low speed until combined and there are no white bits in the mixture.

Transfer the batter to the prepared loaf tin, then sprinkle over the pecans and pumpkin seeds.

Bake for 60–70 minutes, until a skewer inserted into the loaf comes out clean. Remove from the oven, leave to cool in the tin for 10 minutes then turn out onto a wire rack and allow to cool completely. Slice and serve.

PUMP-CHOC BROWNIES

Or should we say, Chocolate Orange-ies? It probably depends on how precisely you swirl the pumpkin and chocolate batters together. But if you squint at the result, it's going to look good regardless. Congratulations.

Makes 9–12

170 g (6 oz) dark chocolate (70% cocoa), chopped

115 g (4 oz) butter

300 g (2 cups) plain (all-purpose) flour

1 teaspoon baking powder

½ teaspoon salt

330 g (1½) cups sugar

4 eggs

1 tablespoon vanilla extract

310 g (1¼ cups) Pumpkin puree, fresh (see page 11) or tinned

60 ml (¼ cup) canola oil

1 teaspoon Pumpkin pie spice (see page 12)

Preheat oven to 180°C (350°F). Line a 33 × 23 cm (13 × 9 in) baking tray with baking paper and set aside.

Place the chocolate and the butter in a bowl, then pop in the microwave and heat for 15 seconds. Stir, then continue to heat and stir until the chocolate and butter are both melted and combined.

Place the flour, baking powder and salt in a bowl and mix to combine. Place the sugar, eggs and vanilla in a separate bowl, then use an electric mixer to beat until pale, about 3–4 minutes. In three batches, add the flour mixture to the wet mixture, stopping and mixing between each addition.

Remove half the batter to a separate bowl. Add the chocolate to one bowl and stir to combine. Add the puree, oil and pumpkin pie spice to the other bowl and stir well.

Pour the chocolate mixture into the prepared tray and smooth the top with a rubber spatula. Then pour the pumpkin mixture over the chocolate in a semi-swirl way. Use a spatula to gently swirl the two mixtures, creating a marbled effect. Transfer to the oven and bake for 35–40 minutes, until cooked and a skewer comes out clean.

Remove from the oven and allow to cool on a wire rack before cutting to your desired size.

PUMPKIN(G) PIE

This dessert is royalty. When you come at the king, you best not miss. Yes, you could buy one ready-made from that store down the road, but making your own from scratch will give you bragging rights for days. Don't mess this up.

✗ ✗

Makes 1 pie

425 g (15 oz) Pumpkin puree, fresh (see page 11) or tinned

1 egg, plus 3 egg yolks

230 g (1 cup) light brown sugar, firmly packed

2 tablespoons plain (all-purpose) flour

1 tablespoon Pumpkin pie spice (see page 12)

310 ml (1¼ cups) evaporated milk

small handful pecans, pumpkin seeds and dried cranberries, to decorate

Pastry

150 g (1 cup) plain (all-purpose) flour

55 g (¼ cup) caster (superfine) sugar

60 g (2 oz) cold unsalted butter, chopped

2 egg yolks

1 tablespoon iced water

To make the pastry, place the flour, sugar and butter in a food processor and pulse to combine. Add the egg yolks and iced water and process until the ingredients just come together, adding a little water if needed. Press the dough into a flat disc shape, cover with plastic wrap and refrigerate for 30 minutes.

Roll out the pastry between two sheets of baking paper to about 3 mm (¹⁄₁₀ in) thick, large enough to line a 20 cm (8 in) loose-based pie tin. Gently press the pastry into the tin, then trim the edge. Chill for a further 30 minutes.

Meanwhile, preheat the oven to 170°C (340°F).

Cover the pastry with baking paper and fill with baking beads or dried beans. Place on a baking tray and bake for 10 minutes. Carefully remove the paper and weights and bake for a further 10 minutes, or until the pastry is cooked through and lightly browned. Set aside to cool.

Increase the oven temperature to 200°C (400°F).

Place the filling ingredients into a large bowl and mix well with a whisk until you have a smooth mixture. Pour the mixture into the case, then transfer to the oven. Cook for 50–60 minutes, until the mixture has set. Remove from the oven and allow to cool. Decorate then serve.

PUMPKIN DONUTS

Not unlike the humble squirrel, stashing away nuts to survive the winter, it's our evolutionary duty to eat as many of these adorable donuts treats as possible in each sitting. Only that way, we may brave the cold months and survive.

✗   ✗

Makes 24

185 g (¾ cup) Pumpkin puree, fresh (see page 11) or tinned

125 ml (½ cup) milk

95 g (½ cup) brown sugar

80 ml (⅓ cup) canola oil

1 egg

1 teaspoon vanilla extract

260 g (1¾ cups) plain (all-purpose) flour

1½ teaspoons Pumpkin pie spice (see page 12)

2 teaspoons baking powder

12 pretzel sticks

60 g (½ cup) chocolate sprinkles

60 ml (¼ cup) chocolate syrup

Glaze
250 g (2 cups) icing (confectioners') sugar

60 ml (¼ cup) milk

Preheat oven to 180°C (350°F). Lightly grease a 24-hole mini-muffin or mini-cupcake pan.

In a bowl, whisk together the pumpkin puree, milk, brown sugar, canola oil, egg and vanilla. In a separate bowl, combine the flour, pumpkin pie spice, baking powder and a pinch of salt. Pour the wet mixture over the dry mixture, then use a wooden spoon to mix until just combined. Divide the batter evenly between the holes in the tray. Transfer to the oven and bake for 10–12 minutes, or until cooked through and a skewer comes out clean.

Remove from the oven and turn out to cool on a wire rack.

To make the glaze, in a bowl mix together the sugar and milk until smooth. Roll the donuts in the glaze and place back on the wire rack to dry.

Place the chocolate sprinkles and syrup in two separate shallow bowls. Dip half of each donuts in the syrup then the sprinkles to coat. Halve each pretzel stick, and insert half a stick into each donuts.

PUMPKIN CUPCAKES

If you want to win hearts and minds on your street
this Halloween, give the first dozen trick-or-treaters
these little homemade pumpkin-frosted masterpieces
as an early bird special. They'll love you for it.

✖   ✖

Makes 12

225 g (1½ cups) plain (all-purpose) flour

2 teaspoons Pumpkin pie spice (see page 12)

1 teaspoon baking powder

½ teaspoon baking soda

115 g (4 oz) butter, softened

185 g (1 cup) brown sugar, lightly packed

2 eggs

250 g (1 cup) Pumpkin puree, fresh (see page 11) or tinned

Frosting

3 tablespoons butter, softened

90 g (⅓ cup) Pumpkin puree, fresh (see page 11) or tinned

½ teaspoon Pumpkin pie spice (see page 12)

310 g (2½ cups) icing (confectioners') sugar

Preheat oven to 180°C (350°F). Line a 12-hole muffin tray with cupcake wrappers.

Sift the flour, pumpkin pie spice, baking powder, baking soda and a pinch of salt into a bowl.

Place the butter and sugar in separate bowl, then use an electric mixer to beat until pale, about 3–4 minutes. Add the eggs, one at a time, mixing well after each addition. Add half the puree, then half the dry ingredients, then the remaining puree and remaining dry ingredients, mixing after each addition.

Divide the batter between the cupcake wrappers. Transfer to the oven and bake for 20–25 minutes, or until a skewer comes out clean. Remove from the oven then allow to cool completely on a wire rack.

To make the frosting, place the butter and puree in a bowl and use a hand mixer to beat until combined. Add the pumpkin pie spice and ½ cup of the sugar and beat again, then continue to add the sugar in batches, until the frosting is the right consistency. Place the frosting into a piping bag and pipe on top of the cooled cupcakes.

PUMPKIN BUTTER

Are you yearning for a churning? Well, that's a shame because it's the 21st century and literally everyone owns a food processor. Use it to make your puree then whip up this spiced pumpkin butter – perfect for schmearing on surfaces both savoury and sweet.

Makes 500 g (1 lb 2 oz)

500 g (2 cups) Pumpkin puree, fresh (see page 11) or tinned

115 g (½ cup) brown sugar

125 ml (½ cup) apple juice

1 teaspoon Pumpkin pie spice (see page 12)

Place all the ingredients into a small heavy-bottomed saucepan over a medium heat. Bring the mixture to the boil, stirring often.

Once the mixture starts to bubble, reduce the heat to low and continue to cook for 20–30 minutes, until thickened, continuing to stir often. Allow to cool completely.

Taste and adjust the level of spice to your liking. Place the butter into an airtight container with a lid.

This spiced pumpkin butter will keep in the fridge for up to two weeks.

PUMPKIN SEED BRITTLE

Nine out of every ten dentists recommend against chomping down on brittle of any kind. Although, we did find one – a single dentist – who confirmed that pumpkin seed brittle is surprisingly good for your teeth. Let's run with that.

✗ ✗

Makes 550 g (1 lb 3 oz)

1 cup fresh pumpkin seeds (from a sugar pumpkin or similar)

550 g (2½ cups) sugar

50 g (1¾ oz) butter, plus extra for greasing

pinch of salt

Preheat the oven to 190°C (375°F). Wash and dry the seeds, ensuring there are no fibres left with them. Spread the seeds out on a baking tray, and toast in the oven for 15 minutes, until lightly roasted. Remove from the oven.

Line a large baking tray with baking paper, then grease with butter.

Combine the sugar and 125 ml (½ cup) water in a small saucepan over a medium heat. Stir until the sugar dissolves, then bring to the boil. Reduce the heat to medium, then continue to cook for 20–25 minutes, until the mixture is a rich golden brown.

Remove from the heat, add a pinch of salt and then stir in the butter until melted and combined. Working quickly, stir in the pumpkin seeds then pour the mixture out onto your prepared tray.

Leave to cool until set then break the brittle into pieces and store in an airtight container.

CANDIED PUMPKIN

De-health-ifying fruit and vegetables is as American as ... well, pumpkin pie. It's the best in the world at taking something from farm to table by way of the sugar mill. These candied pumpkin pieces are a prime example.

×   ×

Makes 300 g (11 oz)

1 kg (2 lb 3 oz) peeled and cleaned pumpkin (winter squash)

550 g (2½ cups) sugar

juice and zest of 2 lemons

1 cinnamon stick (optional)

small knob fresh ginger, peeled and sliced (optional)

3 teaspoons icing sugar

1 teaspoon cornflour (corn starch)

Cut the pumpkin into 15 mm (½ in) cubes. Place into a large saucepan and add the sugar, lemon juice and zest, and the cinnamon and ginger, if using. Give the mixture a stir, then cover and refrigerate overnight, turning over the mixture gently once or twice in that time.

The next day, place a sieve over a bowl, and cover a cooling rack with a sheet of baking paper. Set both aside until needed.

Place the saucepan over a medium heat and bring to a gentle boil. Cook for 10 minutes, then turn off the heat and allow to stand until the mixture has reached room temperature. Repeat this boil-and-cool step, then boil once more. Remove from the heat then use a slotted spoon to transfer the pumpkin into your sieve, discarding the caramel, ginger and cinnamon stick. Discard the liquid.

Lay the pumpkin in a single layer on the prepared cooling rack, then leave to dry for 12 hours, or overnight, turning once or twice.

Mix the icing sugar and cornflour in a small bowl, then sift it over the candy. Toss it all together to coat, then transfer to an airtight container to store.

THE PSL

You know what it stands for: Pumpkin Spiced Latte.
Those who dare deny this holiest of elixirs don't
deserve Fall. They should be excommunicated for
three months of every year to minimise PSL-naysaying
throughout the season.

✗   ✗

Serves 2

500 ml (2 cups) milk of
your choice

2 tablespoons light brown
sugar

60 g (¼ cup) Pumpkin
puree, fresh (see page 11)
or tinned

½ teaspoon Pumpkin pie
spice (see page 12)

2 shots of espresso

canned whipped cream,
to top

Place the milk, sugar, puree and pumpkin pie spice into a
saucepan and place over a medium heat until steaming,
without allowing it to boil. Remove from the heat and add
the espresso.

Divide between two heat-proof glasses or mugs and top with
whipped cream and an extra sprinkle of pumpkin spice.

PUMPKIN -TINI

Has your Thanksgiving become an exercise in delicately avoiding – or endlessly detonating – political landmines? Whatever the answer, you should probably add more booze into the equation.

✕ ✕

Serves 1

1 tablespoon Pumpkin puree, fresh (see page 11) or tinned

60 ml (¼ cup) vodka

60 ml (¼ cup) orange juice

1 teaspoon lemon juice

few drops of orange food colouring (optional)

Chill a martini glass.

Fill a cocktail shaker with ice then add all of the ingredients. Shake vigorously for 30 seconds, then use a fine mesh strainer to strain the cocktail into a chilled martini glass.

Garnish with a paper bat, if you like.

PUMPKIN PIE SHAKE

Some folks wake up as the first light of dawn breaks, perform sun salutations and make themselves a kale and otherwise-obnoxiously-green smoothie. This milkshake is not for these people. It's for us who understand that sugar is the meaning of life.

✕   ✕

Serves 2

3 tablespoons chocolate syrup, plus extra to garnish

1 tablespoon sprinkles

2 large scoops (about 1 cup) vanilla ice cream

250 ml (1 cup) whole milk

60 g (¼ cup) Pumpkin puree, fresh (see page 11) or tinned

½ teaspoon Pumpkin pie spice (see page 12; optional)

canned whipped cream, to top

candy corn, mini pretzels, sprinkles, and candy eyes, to decorate

Smear some chocolate syrup around the edge of two sundae glasses and roll in the sprinkles to coat, then set aside.

Place the chocolate syrup, ice cream, milk, pumpkin puree and spice (if using) into a blender and blitz until smooth.

Divide the milkshake between the prepared glasses.

Top with whipped cream and decorate as you choose.

THINGS TO MAKE

GAUDY PUNCHBOWL

For millennia, gourds have been fashioned into canteens for water, wine and everything in between. It is with this storied history in mind that we're about to turn a big ol' pumpkin into a vessel for some mulled wine so we can get our friends drunk.

What you need for the bowl

1 large pumpkin

Sharp, serrated knife

Heat-proof bowl

What you need for the mulled wine

3 oranges

6 cloves, plus more for garnish

2 bottles red wine

60 ml (¼ cup) brandy

115 g (½ cup) brown sugar

3 cinnamon sticks

4 star anise

Step 1: Carve the vessel

Find a huge-ish pumpkin, big enough to hold an 8-cup capacity bowl. Slice a thin layer off the base to ensure it sits flat on a table. Hollow out the inside of the pumpkin, so that your heat-proof bowl sits inside it comfortably. Set aside.

Step 2: Make the booze

Cut one orange into slices then half-moon slices, then pierce each wedge with 2 cloves to garnish and set aside. Juice the two remaining oranges. Place the juice, wine, brandy, sugar, cinnamon sticks, 6 cloves and star anise into a saucepan. With caution (alcohol is highly flammable, remember), heat over a medium heat until steaming, then reduce the heat to low and cook for a further 5 minutes. The wine will become more richly spiced the longer you simmer it, so taste along the way and remove from the heat when you're happy with the flavour.

Step 3: Serve

Carefully pour the hot punch into the prepared bowl. Ladle the wine into heat-proof glasses, serving with a clove-studded orange slice to garnish. Mull together with friends and enjoy. This amount should serve roughly 10 people.

A CENTREPIECE

It's the ultimate seasonal conversation starter. "Is that a pumpkin in the middle of the table?". "Ornamental, you say?" "Do you have any other weird hobbies? Or mostly just the pumpkin thing?" The possibilities for meaningful discourse are endless.

What you need

1 pumpkin

1 squat vase

floral foam

assorted flowers, leaves, smaller gourds and autumnal detritus

Step 1: Choose your gourd
Pick a large, bright pumpkin to be the star of the show. It needs to be large enough to fit a smaller vase inside.

Step 2: Secure
Cut a thin slice from the base of the pumpkin to ensure it won't roll away. Hollow out the inside in the rough shape of your vase.

Step 3: Fill
Place some soaked floral foam into the vase, and then place the vase into the pumpkin. Now channel your inner overpriced florist. Start to insert your assorted fall foliage – and any decorations you'd like – directly into the foam. Think fall colours. You can place smaller gourds or squashes onto skewers, then feature them within the arrangement. Like wholesome little heads on spikes.

Step 4: Display
To ensure your display takes centre stage, place it on a pedestal in the middle of the table. That could be a velvet cushion, a gallery plinth or a lazy Susan, so long as it's visible to every guest at all times.

Step 5: Bask
Sit back and enjoy the kudos from friends, relatives and the entire internet.

FARM TO TABLE

It ain't much, but it's honest work. Okay, it's more like hard work. Nurturing a crop of gourds is the kind of thing that might take over your life, ruin relationships and create violent feuds with neighbours. But when those first beauties come rolling in, you won't regret a thing.

Step 1: Choose your fighter

You can use the leftover seeds from the pumpkins and gourds you've hollowed out elsewhere in this book. Otherwise, you can find all kinds of seeds in your local garden centre. Choose what will suit your needs, space and local environment. Note that pumpkins used for carving usually have thinner skins and don't taste great. Decide if you want to eat or carve your crop, then go from there.

Step 2: Decide when to plant

The average growing cycle for gourds is 80 to 120 days, so you'll need to decide when you want to harvest them, then count backwards on your calendar to figure out your planting date. Pumpkins grow quicker in the heat of summer.

Step 3: Pick your spot

Pumpkins need to be planted in full sun to maximise the chances of you having a decent haul come harvest time. They also need a lot of space, as the vines stretch out, so allow about 6–9 m (20–30 ft) for your pumpkin patch. Smaller varieties will need a little less space. They also need good drainage, so prepare the soil by tilling and mixing in some organic compost.

Step 4: Planting

If you are planting multiple batches of seeds, space them out, leaving at least 1.2 m (4 ft) between each. Make a little mound, and place 2 or 3 seeds into it before covering with soil. Water the seeds well.

Step 5: Watering

Water regularly, taking your cues from the soil. If it's always wet, don't overwater. If dry, give a good soaking to ensure it reaches the roots. These babies need plenty of water to grow to size, so make it rain.

Step 6: Tending

Once the seedlings have sprouted, you can add compost around the base and spread organic vegetable fertiliser over the top. When the plant begins to grow, you can thin off the weaker ones, leaving the stronger plants to grow and mature. You can also trim off additional shoots or the tops to encourage the existing vines to get nice and strong. There are plenty of insects that will want a taste of your pumpkin patch. Keep an eye out, removing them by hand or with water, keeping pesticide as a last resort.

Step 7: Harvesting

Rejoice, it's time to harvest! Yank out your gourds and feast with friends and family.

PUMPKIN BODY SCRUB

Champagne lifestyle on a lemonade budget? Try Goop-esque skincare with tap water funds. The good news: the beauty industry is morally bankrupt and have normalised extortionate prices for basic skincare. Take the power back – start making your own.

What you need

60 g (¼ cup) Pumpkin puree, fresh (see page 11) or tinned

230 g (1 cup) brown sugar

½ teaspoon Pumpkin pie spice (see page 12)

2 teaspoons vanilla extract

60 ml (¼ cup) olive, sweet almond or argan oil

glass jar, with a lid

sticky labels and pen

Step 1: Mix
Place all of the ingredients in a clean bowl. Mix until well combined.

Step 2: Store
Transfer to a clean glass jar, label with the name and date. Store in the fridge until you are ready to use it.

Step 3: Shower
Next time you shower, bring the jar of body scrub along with you. Scoop out with your hands and scrub in sweeping circular motions, gently exfoliating the skin. Leave for 30 seconds and then rinse off your body.

Step 4: Glow
Once you're out of the shower, admire the preternatural glow coming now from your skin. Return the jar to the fridge for next time.

GOURD MARACAS

For the rhythmically challenged, few instruments feel friendly and inviting. Tambourines come to mind. Triangles strike a chord. Yet only maracas allow an untrained percussionist to flail both arms wildly and still create a fun sound. So, why not make them out of fun little gourds?

What you need

2 small gourds – even-sized and round (one should fit in your palm), with no visible rot

1 cup dried beans

2 smooth dowels for the handles (available from craft or homeware stores)

glue

masking tape

sharp knife

craft paint and paintbrush

shellac spray

Step 1: Cut
Use the knife to carefully cut a thumb-sized hole in the base of each gourd.

Step 2: Scoop
Take any sturdy spoon or safe utensil at your disposal to scrape out the inside of the gourd through the hole. Get as many of the seeds and fibres as you can manage without damaging the outer walls – at least two-thirds.

Step 3: Dry
Leave the hollowed-out gourds to dry overnight somewhere well-ventilated.

Step 4: Beans
The next day or so, poke your finger in to check if the gourds have dried out. If so, insert ½ cup beans into each.

Step 5: Plug
Plug the hole of each gourd with a dowel, then use the glue to seal it into place, and leave to dry completely. Wind some tape around where the pumpkin meets the dowel, for good measure.

Step 6: Paint and shellac
Paint the gourd and handle in bright colours to your liking, then leave to dry. Finish with a layer of shellac to make sure your maracas won't rot, and once again leave until completely dry.

Step 7: Play!
Pick up your new maracas and kick off a fiesta.

PUMPKIN HAIR MASK

For many of us, changes of season signal a full-blown hair meltdown. Use the fruits of fall against the quarterly hurdle it brings with this mask that deep-conditions, adds shine and is a great antidote to dry hair.

What you need

250 g (1 cup) Pumpkin puree, fresh (see page 11) or tinned

2 tablespoons coconut oil (melted)

2 tablespoons plain yoghurt

1 tablespoon honey

a few drops of vitamin E oil (optional)

Step 1: Mix
Mix all your ingredients together in a small bowl.

Step 2: Apply
Apply the mixture by sectioning your damp hair and massaging the mask into the scalp, then working your way down to the roots until you have worked the entire mixture in. Use a wide tooth comb if needed.

Step 3: Cover and chill
Take a plastic shower cap and place it on your head, then wrap a towel on top. Leave the mask to work for 15 minutes.

Step 4: Wash away
When the time is up, wash the mask from your freshly conditioned hair using warm water.

GOURD WATER CANTEEN

Be warned: six months in, this gourd-centric undertaking might start to feel a little Gordian. You'll be in it for the long haul, but the pay-off is well worth it. Canteen, bottle or Chinese gourds work well for this: simply plant, grow, harvest, then begin!

What you need

1 bottle gourd

bleach

water

600 g (1 lb 5 oz) beeswax, plus more for shining

water

tapered cork

saw

Step 1: Choose your gourd
Take your gourd and rub the outside with a 10 per cent bleach solution (1 part bleach, 9 parts water), to prevent rot. You'll need to leave that fella in a cool, dry place for a really, really long time. It can take anywhere from six months to a year.

Step 2: Clean it up
When the gourd is ready (it will be light and sound hollow when tapped), you're ready to clean it. Using another 10 per cent bleach solution, clean the outside of the gourd, using a soft scrubber to remove any outer layers or mould. Leave overnight to dry.

Step 3: Cut and clean again
Trace the shape of the small end of your cork around the neck, then use a small hand-held saw to cut the hole. Remove the top then use a something with a long handle to break up and pull out the seeds and fibres from inside. Once that's done, you can put some small stones or baking beads inside and swirl them to dislodge the rest of the gourd guts, then shake out all the stones.

Step 4: Wax on
Melt a third of the beeswax, pour it into the hole and swirl it around, then pour out, discarding the excess wax. Let cool, then repeat the process twice more until the inside is fully coated.

Step 5: Drinking time
Use a small knife to tidy up the hole, checking to make sure the cork fits snugly. You can shine that baby up with a thin layer of beeswax, and then it's ready to use.

ANIMAL SNACK-O'-LANTERN

With this seasonal bird feeder, your backyard will become a fabulous retreat for the most beautiful birdlife in the area. To dissuade any wildlife from coming to rely on it, take down and compost your creation once it's emply and the pumpkin is fading.

What you need

small pumpkin or gourd

sharp knife

twine

6–8 decent-sized twigs

Step 1: Make the feeder

Take a fresh pumpkin or gourd and cut it in half. There's no real need to hollow them out, as the whole pumpkin is edible, but if you wanted the seeds for something else, such as a making delicious Pumpkin seed brittle (see page 40) or to Pumpkin seed loaf (see page 28), then salvage them. Use a sharp knife to poke 8 evenly spaced holes around the pumpkin, each about 2 cm (¾ in) from the cut edge. Push your twigs into these holes. Cut two long pieces of twine and tie one end of the twine around one twig, and the other end around the next, then repeat on the opposite side so that they are evenly balanced.

Step 2: Source your feed

You can rustle up your own seed mix from pet stores or outdoor centres, but it's just as easy to make at home. You can toss together animal friendly ingredients, just make sure to check what local animals can and can't eat before you start.

Step 3: Hang, chill and enjoy

Find a nice spot for your feeder – somewhere you can see it and that's high up, away from the reach of domestic animals. The arms of a nice tree branch are perfect. Use the twine to hook the feeder onto the branch, adjusting the twine length if needed so that the pumpkin sits level. Fill it with some feed. Step back and watch as local birds flock to your gourd like something from a bootleg Disney film.

MAKE COMPOST

We are made from earth, and to earth we will return. Same goes for gourds! Or it should, at least. Once a well-loved pumpkin has reached the end of the line, give its life one last purpose by transforming it to compost. It's the circle of composting life, baby.

Composting Yays

your old pumpkin and gourds

fruit and vegetable scraps

crushed eggshells

tea and coffee grounds

grass and plant cuttings

old flowers

straw

newspaper and cardboard

dry leaves

untreated wood shavings and sawdust

Composting Nays

cooking fats and oils

butter and dairy

meat and bones

pet waste and cat litter

aggressive weeds

weeds with seeds

diseased plants or cuttings

Halloween decorations

Step 1: Crunch the numbers

Choose where you'll put your compost, which will likely be guided by how much outdoor space you have. Smaller backyards are suited to tumbling or static composting bins, but if you have a sprawling property – where the occasional stench won't reach the homestead – a compost pile would be the way to go.

Step 2: Composting Yays

Knowing what can go into your compost is essential to keeping it healthy and happy. Treat it with the respect it deserves.

Step 3: Composting Nays

Avoid tossing forbidden items into your compost. We're trying to create organic fertiliser here, not a local hazmat emergency.

Step 4: Layer up

For reasons that are too complicated to explain – science reasons – it's important you layer your compost. Start with some twigs or mulch to allow some air to circulate. Then layer green and then brown material on top. Keep the pile covered to help the process, and turn the compost over every couple of weeks using a trusty pitchfork.

Step 5: Enjoy the stinky fruits of your labour

The compost is ready when it's dark brown and crumbly. This can take a few months, depending on what scale you're working to. Distribute it onto your lawn, flower and vegetable beds, or mix with potting soil.

Black area is the carve-out area

Black area is the carve-out area

Published in 2023 by Smith Street Books
Naarm (Melbourne) | Australia
smithstreetbooks.com

ISBN: 978-1-9227-5402-8

Smith Street Books respectfully acknowledges the Wurundjeri People of the
Kulin Nation, who are the Traditional Owners of the land on which we work,
and we pay our respects to their Elders past and present.

Publisher: Paul McNally
Text: Patrick Boyle and Aisling Coughlan
Editor: Aisling Coughlan
Design: George Saad
Design layout: Heather Menzies, Studio31 Graphics
Proofreader: Rosanna Dutson

Printed & bound in China by C&C Offset Printing Co., Ltd.

Book 278
10 9 8 7 6 5 4 3 2 1